12.95

Other Books by Jane Kenyon

FROM ROOM TO ROOM

TWENTY POEMS OF ANNA AKHMATOVA
(Translation)

THE BOAT OF QUIET HOURS

LET EVENING COME

Constance

POEMS BY JANE KENYON

GRAYWOLF PRESS, SAINT PAUL

Many of these poems first appeared in magazines: *The Atlantic Monthly:* "Moving the Frame"; *Country Journal:* "August Rain, after Haying," and "Not Here"; *The Gettysburg Review:* "Insomnia at the Solstice" and "Potato"; *Harvard Magazine:* "Notes from the Other Side" and "Otherwise"; *The Iowa Review:* "Chrysanthemums" and "Climb"; *The New Criterion:* "In Memory of Jack" and "Windfalls"; *Partisan Review:* "Sleepers in Jaipur"; *The Boston Phoenix:* "Winter Lambs"; *Ploughshares:* "The Argument"; *Pequod:* "The Stroller"; *New Virginia Review:* "Peonies at Dusk"; *Virginia Quarterly Review:* "Biscuit," "History: Hamden, Connecticut" (later changed to "A Portion of History"), "Not Writing," "The Secret," and "Three Small Oranges." "Gettysburg: July 1, 1863," "Back," "Coats," and "Pharaoh" first appeared in *The New Yorker.* "Having It Out with Melancholy" first appeared in *Poetry,* © 1992, The Modern Poetry Association.

The author thanks the John Simon Guggenheim Foundation for the support and encouragement so critical to the completion of this book.

Also, perpetual thanks go to Donald Hall, Alice Mattison, and Joyce Peseroff.

Publication of this volume is made possible in part by a grant provided by the Minnesota State Arts Board through an appropriation by the Minnesota State Legislature, and by a grant from the National Endowment for the Arts. Additional support has been provided by the Andrew W. Mellon Foundation, the Lila Wallace-Reader's Digest Fund, the McKnight Foundation, the Dayton-Hudson Foundation for Dayton's and Target stores, the Cowles Media Foundation, the General Mills Foundation, and other generous contributions from foundations, corporations, and individuals. Graywolf Press is a member agency of United Arts, Saint Paul. To these organizations and individuals who make our work possible, we offer heartfelt thanks.

Published by G R A Y W O L F P R E S S
2402 University Avenue, Suite 203
Saint Paul, Minnesota 55114
All rights reserved.
Printed in the United States of America.

6 8 9 7

Library of Congress Cataloging-in-Publication Data
Kenyon, Jane.
Constance : poems / by Jane Kenyon.
p.   cm.
ISBN 1-55597-195-4 (cloth) – ISBN 1-55597-196-2 (paper)
I. Title.
PS3561.E554C6 1993
811'.54–dc20   93–242

PERKINS, EVER FOR PERKINS

Contents

IV. *"Watch Ye, Watch Ye"*

FROM PSALM 139
"O Lord, thou hast searched me . . ."

Whither shall I go from thy spirit?
   or whither shall I flee from thy presence?

If I ascend up into heaven, thou art there:
   if I make my bed in hell, behold, thou art there.

If I take the wings of the morning,
   and dwell in the uttermost parts of the sea;

Even there shall thy hand lead me,
   and thy right hand shall hold me.

If I say, Surely the darkness shall cover me;
   even the night shall be light about me.

Yea, the darkness hideth not from thee;
   but the night shineth as the day:
    the darkness and the light are both alike to thee. . . .

I

The Progress of a Beating Heart

August Rain, after Haying

Through sere trees and beheaded
grasses the slow rain falls.
Hay fills the barn; only the rake
and one empty wagon are left
in the field. In the ditches
goldenrod bends to the ground.

Even at noon the house is dark.
In my room under the eaves
I hear the steady benevolence
of water washing dust
raised by the haying
from porch and car and garden
chair. We are shorn
and purified, as if tonsured.

The grass resolves to grow again,
receiving the rain to that end,
but my disordered soul thirsts
after something it cannot name.

The Stroller

It was copen blue, strong and bright,
and the metal back looked like caning
on a chair. The peanut-shaped tray
had a bar with sliding beads:
red, yellow, blue, green, white.
It was hard for Mother to push the stroller
on the sandy shoulders of the road.

Sitting in the stroller
in the driveway of the new house
on a morning in early spring, trees
leafing out, I could hear cows
lowing in their stalls across the road,
and see geese hissing and flapping
at a sheep that wandered too close
to the goslings. From the stroller I surveyed
my new domain like a dowager queen.
When something pleased me I kicked
my feet and spun the bright beads.
Spittle dropped from my lower lip
like a spider plunging on its filament.

1991

Mother is moving; we're sorting
through fifty years' accumulations —
a portfolio of Father's drawings
from his brief career in Architecture
School, exercises in light and shadow,
vanishing point; renderings of acanthus
cornices, gargoyles. . . . Then I come upon
a drawing of my stroller, precisely to scale,
just as I remember it.

And here is a self-portrait, looser,
where he wears the T-shirt whose stripes
I know were red and white
although the drawing is pencil.
Beside Father, who sits in a blue chair
that I remember, by a bookcase I remember,
under a lamp I remember, is the empty stroller.

1951

He was forty-seven, a musician
who took other jobs to get by,
a dreamer, a reader, a would-be farmer
with weak lungs from many pneumonias

and from playing cocktail piano
late in smoky bars. On weekend mornings
we crept around so he could sleep until ten.

When he came home from his day-job
at the bookstore, I untied his shoes.
I waited all day to untie them,
wanting no other happiness. I was four.
He never went to town without a suit
and tie, a linen handkerchief
in his pocket, and his shoes
were good leather, the laces themselves
leather. I loved the rich pungency
of his brown, well-shined, warm shoes.

1 9 5 9

Mother took in sewing.
One by one Ann Arbor's bridge club
ladies found her. They pulled into our drive
in their Thunderbirds and Cadillacs
as I peered down between muslin curtains
from my room. I lay back on the bed, thinking
of nothing in particular, until they went
away. When I came downstairs the scent
of cigarettes and perfume persisted in the air.

One of them I liked. She took
her two dachshunds everywhere
on a bifurcated leash; they hopped comically
up the porch steps and into our house.
She was Italian, from Modena, displaced,
living in Ann Arbor as the wife
of a Chrysler executive. She never wore
anything but beige or gray knits.
She was six feet tall and not ashamed of it,
with long, loose red hair held back
by tortoiseshell combs. She left cigarette
butts in the ashtray with bright red
striated crescents on them.

She was different from the others,
attached to my mother in the way
European women are attached
to their dressmakers and hairdressers.
When she travelled abroad
she brought back classical recordings
and perfume. I thought I would not mind
being like Marcella, though I recognized
that she was lonely. Her husband travelled
frequently, and she had a son
living in Florence who never came "home."
His enterprises were obscure. . . .
Marcella had her dogs, her solitude,

her elegance – at once sedate and slightly
wild – and, it seemed, a new car every time
the old one got dirty, a luxury
to which she seemed oblivious.

1991

Disturbed but full of purpose, we push
Father's indifferent drawings into the trash.
Mother saves the self-portrait and the acanthus
cornice. I save only the rendering
of the stroller, done on tracing paper, diaphanous.

Looking at it
is like looking into a mirror
and seeing your own eyes and someone else's
eyes as well, strange to you
but benign, curious, come
to interrogate your wounds, the progress
of your beating heart.

The Argument

On the way to the village store
I drive through a down-draft
from the neighbor's chimney.
Woodsmoke tumbles from the eaves
backlit by sun, reminding me
of the fire and sulfur of Grandmother's
vengeful God, the one who disapproves
of jeans and shorts for girls,
dancing, strong waters, and adultery.

A moment later the smoke enters
the car, although the windows are tight,
insinuating that I might, like Judas,
and the foolish virgins, and the rich
young man, have been made for unquenchable
fire. God will need something to burn
if the fire is to be unquenchable.

"All things work together for the good
for those who love God," she said
to comfort me at Uncle Hazen's funeral,
where Father held me up to see
the maroon gladiolus that trembled
as we approached the bier, the elaborate
shirred satin, brass fittings, anything,

oh, anything but Uncle's squelched
and made-up face.
"No! NO! How is it good to be dead?"
I cried afterward, wild-eyed and flushed.
"God's ways are not our ways,"
she said then out of pity
and the wish to forestall the argument.

Biscuit

The dog has cleaned his bowl
and his reward is a biscuit,
which I put in his mouth
like a priest offering the host.

I can't bear that trusting face!
He asks for bread, expects
bread, and I in my power
might have given him a stone.

Not Writing

A wasp rises to its papery
nest under the eaves
where it daubs

at the gray shape,
but seems unable
to enter its own house.

Windfalls

The storm is moving on, and as the wind
rises, the oaks and pines let go
of all the snow on their branches,
an abrupt change of heart,
and the air turns utterly white.

Woooh, says the wind, and I stop
where I am, put out my arms
and look upward, allowing
myself to disappear. It is good
to be here, and not here. . . .

I see fresh cloven prints
under the apple tree, where deer come
nosing for windfalls. They must be
near me now, and having stopped
when I stopped, begin to move again.

II

Tell me how to bear myself...

A D R I E N N E R I C H

Having it Out with Melancholy

If many remedies are prescribed
for an illness, you may be certain
that the illness has no cure.

A.P. Chekhov
The Cherry Orchard

1 FROM THE NURSERY

When I was born, you waited
behind a pile of linen in the nursery,
and when we were alone, you lay down
on top of me, pressing
the bile of desolation into every pore.

And from that day on
everything under the sun and moon
made me sad — even the yellow
wooden beads that slid and spun
along a spindle on my crib.

You taught me to exist without gratitude.
You ruined my manners toward God:
"We're here simply to wait for death;
the pleasures of earth are overrated."

I only appeared to belong to my mother,
to live among blocks and cotton undershirts
with snaps; among red tin lunch boxes

and report cards in ugly brown slipcases.
I was already yours – the anti-urge,
the mutilator of souls.

2 BOTTLES

Elavil, Ludiomil, Doxepin,
Norpramin, Prozac, Lithium, Xanax,
Wellbutrin, Parnate, Nardil, Zoloft.
The coated ones smell sweet or have
no smell; the powdery ones smell
like the chemistry lab at school
that made me hold my breath.

3 SUGGESTION FROM A FRIEND

You wouldn't be so depressed
if you really believed in God.

4 OFTEN

Often I go to bed as soon after dinner
as seems adult
(I mean I try to wait for dark)

in order to push away
from the massive pain in sleep's
frail wicker coracle.

5 ONCE THERE WAS LIGHT

Once, in my early thirties, I saw
that I was a speck of light in the great
river of light that undulates through time.

I was floating with the whole
human family. We were all colors — those
who are living now, those who have died,
those who are not yet born. For a few

moments I floated, completely calm,
and I no longer hated having to exist.

Like a crow who smells hot blood
you came flying to pull me out
of the glowing stream.
"I'll hold you up. I never let my dear
ones drown!" After that, I wept for days.

6 IN AND OUT

The dog searches until he finds me
upstairs, lies down with a clatter
of elbows, puts his head on my foot.

Sometimes the sound of his breathing
saves my life – in and out, in
and out; a pause, a long sigh. . . .

7 PARDON

A piece of burned meat
wears my clothes, speaks
in my voice, dispatches obligations
haltingly, or not at all.
It is tired of trying
to be stouthearted, tired
beyond measure.

We move on to the monoamine
oxidase inhibitors. Day and night
I feel as if I had drunk six cups
of coffee, but the pain stops

abruptly. With the wonder
and bitterness of someone pardoned
for a crime she did not commit
I come back to marriage and friends,
to pink fringed hollyhocks; come back
to my desk, books, and chair.

8 CREDO

Pharmaceutical wonders are at work
but I believe only in this moment
of well-being. Unholy ghost,
you are certain to come again.

Coarse, mean, you'll put your feet
on the coffee table, lean back,
and turn me into someone who can't
take the trouble to speak; someone
who can't sleep, or who does nothing
but sleep; can't read, or call
for an appointment for help.

There is nothing I can do
against your coming.
When I awake, I am still with thee.

9 WOOD THRUSH

High on Nardil and June light
I wake at four,
waiting greedily for the first
note of the wood thrush. Easeful air
presses through the screen
with the wild, complex song
of the bird, and I am overcome

by ordinary contentment.
What hurt me so terribly
all my life until this moment?
How I love the small, swiftly
beating heart of the bird
singing in the great maples;
its bright, unequivocal eye.

Litter

I poured the unused coffee grounds
from the paper filter back
into the can. I was too rattled
to spoon the dry Cream of Wheat
back into the packet, so I threw it away.

The neighbor who rushed over
had straightened the bedcovers.
The violets were dry; I watered them.

I picked up blue plastic syringe
tips, strips of white tape,
and the backing from bandages
that the EMTs had dropped in haste.

Now curtains lift and fall
in windows I've never before seen open.

Chrysanthemums

The doctor averted his eyes
while the diagnosis fell on us,
as though the picture of the girl
hiding from her dog
had suddenly fallen off the wall.
We were speechless all the way home.
The light seemed strange.

A weekend of fear and purging...
Determined to work, he packed his
dictaphone, a stack of letters,
and a roll of stamps. At last the day
of scalpels, blood, and gauze arrived.

Eyes closed, I lay on his tightly-made
bed, waiting. From the hallway I heard
an old man, whose nurse was helping him
to walk: "That Howard Johnson's. It's
nothing but the same thing over and over
again."

        "That's right. It's nothing special."

Late in the afternoon, when slanting
sun betrayed a wad of dust under the bed-
side stand, I heard the sound of casters
and footsteps slowing down.
The attendants asked me to leave the room

while they moved him onto the bed,
and the door remained closed a long time.

Evening came. . . .
While he dozed, fitfully, still stupefied
by anaesthetics, I tried to read,
my feet propped on the rails of the bed.
Odette's chrysanthemums
were revealed to me, ranks of them
in the house where Swann, jealousy
constricting his heart, made late night calls.

And while I read, pausing again
and again to look at him, the smell
of chrysanthemums sent by friends
wavered from the sill, mixing
with the smells of drastic occasions
and disinfected sheets.

He was too out of it
to press the bolus for medication.
Every eight minutes, when he could have
more, I pressed it, and morphine dripped
from the vial in the locked box
into his arm. I made a hive
of eight minute cells
where he could sleep without pain,

or beyond caring about pain.

Over days the IVs came out,
and freedom came back to him —
walking, shaving, sitting in a chair.
The most ordinary gestures seemed
cause for celebration.
Hazy with analgesics, he read
the *Boston Globe,* and began to talk
on the telephone.

Once the staples were out,
and we had the discharge papers
in hand, I brought him home, numbed up
for the trip. He dozed in the car,
woke, and looked with astonishment
at the hills, gold and quince
under October sun, a sight so
overwhelming that we began to cry,
he first, and then I.

Climb

From the porch of our house we can see
Mt. Kearsarge, the huge, black-green
presence that tells us where we are,
and what the weather is going to be.
By night we see the red beacon
on the fire warden's tower, by day
the tower itself, minute with distance.

Yesterday I climbed it with a friend
just home from the hospital.
She'd thought the second coming was at hand,
and found herself in a private
room, tastefully appointed, on a ward
she couldn't leave.

We talked and panted, stopped to look
at the undersides of sage and pink
opalescent mushrooms. Our shirts
were wet with effort.

At last we sprawled on the gray granite
ledges, with veins and blotches of pink,
and silver-green lichen, growing like fur.
We looked for our houses; shreds of clouds
floated between our heads; and we saw from above
the muscular shoulders of a patient hawk.

Back

We try a new drug, a new combination
of drugs, and suddenly
I fall into my life again

like a vole picked up by a storm
then dropped three valleys
and two mountains away from home.

I can find my way back. I know
I will recognize the store
where I used to buy milk and gas.

I remember the house and barn,
the rake, the blue cups and plates,
the Russian novels I loved so much,

and the black silk nightgown
that he once thrust
into the toe of my Christmas stocking.

Moving the Frame

Impudent spring has come
since your chest rose and fell
for the last time, bringing
the push and ooze of budding peonies,
with ants crawling over them
exuberantly.

I have framed the picture
from your obituary. It must have been
taken on a hot graduation day:
You're wearing your academic robes
— how splendid they were —
and your hair and beard are curly
with sweat. The tassel sways. . . .
No matter how I move your face
around my desk,
your eyes don't meet my eyes.

There was one hard night
while your breath became shallower
and shallower, and then
you were gone from us. A person
simply vanishes! I came home
and fell deeply asleep for a long
time, but I woke up again.

Fear of Death Awakens Me

...or it's a cloud-shadow passing over Tuckerman Ravine, darkening the warm ledges and alpine vegetation, then moving on. Sunlight reasserts itself, and that dark, moving lane is like something that never happened, something misremembered, dreamed in anxious sleep.

Or it's like swimming unexpectedly into cold water in a spring-fed pond. Fear locates in my chest, instant and profound, and I speed up my stroke, or turn back the way I came, hoping to avoid more cold.

III

Peonies at Dusk

Winter Lambs

All night snow came upon us
with unwavering intent —
small flakes not meandering
but driving thickly down. We woke
to see the yard, the car and road
heaped unrecognizably.

The neighbors' ewes are lambing
in this stormy weather. Three
lambs born yesterday, three more
expected . . .
                    Felix the ram looked
proprietary in his separate pen
while fatherhood accrued to him.
The panting ewes regarded me
with yellow-green, small-
pupiled eyes.

I have a friend who is pregnant —
plans gone awry — and not altogether
pleased. I don't say she should
be pleased. We are creation's
property, its particles, its clay
as we fall into this life,
agree or disagree.

Not Here

Searching for pillowcases trimmed
with lace that my mother-in-law
once made, I open the chest of drawers
upstairs to find that mice
have chewed the blue and white linen
dishtowels to make their nest,
and bedded themselves
among embroidered dresser scarves
and fingertip towels.

Tufts of fibers, droppings like black
caraway seeds, and the stains of birth
and afterbirth give off the strong
unforgettable attar of mouse
that permeates an old farmhouse
on humid summer days.

A couple of hickory nuts
roll around as I lift out
the linens, while a hail of black
sunflower shells
falls on the pillowcases,
yellow with age, but intact.
I'll bleach them and hang them in the sun
to dry. There's almost no one left
who knows how to crochet lace. . . .

The bright-eyed squatters are not here.
They've scuttled out to the fields
for summer, as they scuttled in
for winter – along the wall, from chair
to skirted chair, making themselves
flat and scarce while the cat
dozed with her paws in the air,
and we read the mail
or evening paper, unaware.

Coats

I saw him leaving the hospital
with a woman's coat over his arm.
Clearly she would not need it.
The sunglasses he wore could not
conceal his wet face, his bafflement.

As if in mockery the day was fair,
and the air mild for December. All the same
he had zipped his own coat and tied
the hood under his chin, preparing
for irremediable cold.

In Memory of Jack

Once, coming down the long hill
into Andover on an autumn night
just before deer season, I stopped
the car abruptly to avoid a doe.

She stood, head down, perhaps twenty
feet away, her legs splayed
as if she meant to stand her ground.

For a long moment she looked
at the car, then bolted right at it,
glancing off the hood with a crash,
into a field of corn stubble.

So I rushed at your illness, your
suffering and death—the bright
lights of annihilation and release.

Insomnia at the Solstice

The quicksilver song
of the wood thrush spills
downhill from ancient maples
at the end of the sun's single most
altruistic day. The woods grow dusky
while the bird's song brightens.

Reading to get sleepy . . . Rabbit
Angstrom knows himself so well,
why isn't he a better man?
I turn out the light, and rejoice
in the sound of high summer, and in air
on bare shoulders — *dolce, dolce* —
no blanket, or even a sheet.
A faint glow remains over the lake.

Now come wordless contemplations
on love and death, worry about
money, and the resolve to have the vet
clean the dog's teeth, though
he'll have to anaesthetize him.

An easy rain begins, drips off
the edge of the roof, onto the tin
watering can. A vast irritation rises. . . .
I turn and turn, try one pillow,
two, think of people who have no beds.

A car hisses by on wet macadam.
Then another. The room turns
gray by insensible degrees. The thrush
begins again its outpouring of silver
to rich and poor alike, to the just
and the unjust.

The dog's wet nose appears
on the pillow, pressing lightly,
decorously. He needs to go out.
All right cleverhead, let's declare
a new day.
                    Washing up, I say
to the face in the mirror,
"You're still here! How you bored me
all night, and now I'll have
to entertain you all day. . . . "

Peonies at Dusk

White peonies blooming along the porch
send out light
while the rest of the yard grows dim.

Outrageous flowers as big as human
heads! They're staggered
by their own luxuriance: I had
to prop them up with stakes and twine.

The moist air intensifies their scent,
and the moon moves around the barn
to find out what it's coming from.

In the darkening June evening
I draw a blossom near, and bending close
search it as a woman searches
a loved one's face.

The Secret

In a glass case marked "Estate Jewelry"
I see a ring that seems familiar,
remembered, though I've never seen
anything like it.

I ask the clerk, stout and garrulous
·behind the counter, to take it out.

The honeybee, with opal body, garnet
head, and golden wings, slides past
my knuckle burled with middle age.

That one antenna is broken
only endears it to me. Still
it climbs into the flower's throat,
and flies, heavy with nectar, back
to its queen. . . .

For weeks I have felt on the point
of learning a mystery, but now
my agitation has dropped away.

Watch Ye, Watch Ye

and be ready to meet me,
for lo, I come at noonday.
Fear ye not, fear ye not
for with my hand I will lead you on,
and safely I'll guide your little boat
beyond this vale of sorrow.

SHAKER HYMN

Three Small Oranges

My old flannel nightgown, the elbows out,
one shoulder torn . . . Instead of putting it
away with the clean wash, I cut it up
for rags, removing the arms and opening
their seams, scissoring across the breast
and upper back, then tearing the thin
cloth of the body into long rectangles.
Suddenly an immense sadness . . .

Making supper, I listen to news
from the war, of torture where the air
is black at noon with burning oil,
and of a market in Baghdad, bombed
by accident, where yesterday an old man
carried in his basket a piece of fish
wrapped in paper and tied with string,
and three small hard green oranges.

A Portion of History

The sweet breath of someone's laundry
spews from a dryer vent. A screen door
slams. "Carry it?" – a woman's voice –
"You're going to *carry* it!?" Now I hear
the sound of casters on the sidewalk.

Car doors close softly, engines
turn over and catch. A boy on his bike
delivers papers. I hear the smack
of the *New York Times* in its blue plastic
sheath, hitting the wooden porches.

In the next street a garbage truck cries out.
A woman jogs by, thrusting a child
in a stroller ahead of her, her arms
straight as shafts, the baby's fair
head bobbing wildly on its frail stem.

Potato

In haste one evening while making dinner
I threw away a potato that was spoiled
on one end. The rest would have been

redeemable. In the yellow garbage pail
it became the consort of coffee grounds,
banana skins, carrot peelings.
I pitched it onto the compost
where steaming scraps and leaves
return, like bodies over time, to earth.

When I flipped the fetid layers with a hay
fork to air the pile, the potato turned up
unfailingly, as if to revile me —

looking plumper, firmer, resurrected
instead of disassembling. It seemed to grow
until I might have made shepherd's pie
for a whole hamlet, people who pass the day
dropping trees, pumping gas, pinning
hand-me-down clothes on the line.

Sleepers in Jaipur

A mango moon climbs the dark
blue sky. In the gutters of a market
a white, untethered cow browses
the day's leavings – wilted greens,
banana pecls, spilt rice,
a broken basket.

The sleepers, oh, so many sleepers . . .
They lie on rush mats in their hot
stick hut. The man and woman
want to love wildly, uproariously;
instead, they are quiet and efficient
in the dark. Bangles ring
as his mother stirs in her sleep.

Who can say what will come of
the quickening and slowing
of their breaths on each others'
necks, of their deep shudders?
Another sleeper, a gift of God,
ribs and shoulders to be clothed
in flesh . . .

In the dusty garden the water
she carried from the well in a jug
balanced on her black hair
stares back at the moon
from its cool terra cotta urn.

Gettysburg: July 1, 1863

The young man, hardly more
than a boy, who fired the shot
had looked at him with an air
not of anger but of concentration,
as if he were surveying a road,
or feeding a length of wood into a saw:
It had to be done just so.

The bullet passed through
his upper chest, below the collar bone.
The pain was not what he might
have feared. Strangely exhilarated
he staggered out of the pasture
and into a grove of trees.

He pressed and pressed
the wound, trying to stanch
the blood, but he could only press
what he could reach, and he could
not reach his back, where the bullet
had exited.
       He lay on the earth
smelling the leaves and mosses,
musty and damp and cool
after the blaze of open afternoon.

How good the earth smelled,
as it had when he was a boy
hiding from his father,
who was intent on strapping him
for doing his chores
late one time too many.

A cowbird razzed from a rail fence.
It isn't mockery, he thought,
no malice in it . . . just a noise.
Stray bullets nicked the oaks
overhead. Leaves and splinters fell.

Someone near him groaned.
But it was his own voice he heard.
His fingers and feet tingled,
the roof of his mouth,
and the bridge of his nose. . . .

He became dry, dry, and thought
of Christ, who said, *I thirst.*
His man-smell, the smell of his hair
and skin, his sweat, the salt smell
of his cock and the little ferny hairs
that two women had known

left him, and a sharp, almost sweet
smell began to rise from his open mouth
in the warm shade of the oaks.
A streak of sun climbed the rough
trunk of a tree, but he did not
see it with his open eye.

Pharaoh

"The future ain't what it used to be,"
said the sage of the New York Yankees
as he pounded his mitt, releasing
the red dust of the infield
into the harshly illuminated evening air.

Big hands. Men with big hands
make things happen. The surgeon,
when I asked how big your tumor was,
held forth his substantial fist
with its globed class ring.

Home again, we live as charily as strangers.
Things are off: Touch rankles, food
is not good. Even the kindness of friends
turns burdensome; their flowers sadden
us, so many and so fair.

I woke in the night to see your
diminished bulk lying beside me –
you on your back, like a sarcophagus
as your feet held up the covers. . . .
The things you might need in the next
life surrounded you – your comb and glasses,
water, a book and a pen.

Otherwise

I got out of bed
on two strong legs.
It might have been
otherwise. I ate
cereal, sweet
milk, ripe, flawless
peach. It might
have been otherwise.
I took the dog uphill
to the birch wood.
All morning I did
the work I love.

At noon I lay down
with my mate. It might
have been otherwise.
We ate dinner together
at a table with silver
candlesticks. It might
have been otherwise.
I slept in a bed
in a room with paintings
on the walls, and
planned another day
just like this day.
But one day, I know,
it will be otherwise.

Notes from the Other Side

I divested myself of despair
and fear when I came here.

Now there is no more catching
one's own eye in the mirror,

there are no bad books, no plastic,
no insurance premiums, and of course

no illness. Contrition
does not exist, nor gnashing

of teeth. No one howls as the first
clod of earth hits the casket.

The poor we no longer have with us.
Our calm hearts strike only the hour,

and God, as promised, proves
to be mercy clothed in light.

A Note About the Author

Jane Kenyon was born in Ann Arbor and graduated from the University of Michigan. She is the author of three previous collections of poetry, including *From Room to Room* (Alice James Books, 1978), *The Boat of Quiet Hours* (Graywolf, 1986) and *Let Evening Come* (Graywolf, 1990), and has translated the poetry of Anna Akhmatova (Ally/The Eighties Press, 1985). Her poems have appeared in many magazines including *The New Yorker, The Paris Review, The New Republic, The Atlantic Monthly, Ploughshares*, and *Poetry*.

Jane Kenyon died from leukemia in 1995.

Cover art: *Constance,* Albert Pinkham Ryder,
1896, Oil on Canvas, Abraham Shuman Fund.
Courtesy, Museum of Fine Arts, Boston.
Author photo: Donald Hall.
This book was designed by Tree Swenson.
It is set in Bembo type by The Typeworks
and manufactured by Thomson-Shore
on acid-free paper.